The Life Cycle of a

bullfrog

by Julian May
photographs by Allan Roberts
A CREATIVE EDUCATION MINI BOOK

 Distributed Exclusively by
CHILDRENS PRESS, CHICAGO

ISBN: 0-87191-233-3
Library of Congress Catalog Card Number: 73-1186

Contents

the
life cycle
of a
bullfrog

frog eggs

In springtime, when the weather is warm, the frogs begin to sing. They live in city ponds and lagoons, and in suburban lakes and bogs. They live in wilderness forests and man-made cattle tanks. The small frogs chirp, the medium-sized ones croak. And the largest North American frog of all, the bullfrog, has a loud, deep grunt.

It seems to say, *"Jug-o-rum!"*

The male frogs are calling, seeking mates. The females come looking for them. A pair of frogs go to water, or to some other damp place. She lays her eggs and he pours male cells over them to fertilize them. Only if the eggs are fertilized can they change into tadpoles, or young frogs.

It is in spring, during the mating season, that we are most likely to see bullfrogs. They travel about seeking an uncrowded place to lay their eggs.

Most frog eggs are soft, like jelly. They have no shells. If they become dry, the tiny animals growing inside would die. This is why most frog eggs, like those in the picture, on page 6, are laid in water.

Each bullfrog mother lays between 10,000 and 20,000 eggs. They float on the water, held in a clear, jelly-like material. Not all of the eggs will hatch. Fish, turtles, and other water animals will probably eat some of them.

tadpoles

Bullfrog eggs hatch within 5 to 20 days. The hatching happens more quickly if the water is warm. And the tadpoles will grow more quickly in warm places than in cold ones.

Newly hatched tadpoles are blackish, egg-shaped little creatures with wiggling tails that help them swim. They have no legs. Like fish, they breathe with gills and would die if taken from the water.

At first, the tadpoles stay together in very shallow water. If an enemy comes, it is confused by the large numbers of young and may not eat very many. Still, many of them do not survive the first weeks of life.

The tadpoles have small mouths suited to eating tiny plants that grow in the water. They nibble away at the living green scum that coats pebbles and twigs in the pond. They grow larger and larger.

Bullfrog tadpoles grow much larger than those of other frogs. They may become more than six inches long where there is plenty of food.

As it grows, the tadpole becomes lighter in color—olive-green with light and dark spots. The coloring helps to camouflage the tadpole when it lies quietly on the bottom of a pond or stream. All through its first summer, the bullfrog tadpole lives the life of a fish.

The picture shows the large bullfrog tadpole as it would appear at the end of a southern summer. Its body is oval, its tail long and powerful. There is nothing to suggest that this creature will turn into a frog. It does not resemble its parents at all.

Scientists call this kind of young animal a *larva*. Many insects and crustaceans also have larval young. So do some fishes, such as eels.

In cold climates, the bullfrog tadpole must hibernate, or fall into a deep sleep, during winter. It is a "cold-blooded" animal. This means that its body takes on the temperature of the water around it. The tadpole cannot move or feed in very cold water. So it buries itself in the mud and sleeps until spring.

In warm climates, bullfrog tadpoles stay active all winter long.

metamorphosis

When the tadpole has reached its full growth, its body starts to change. Look at the tadpole on page 14. It is growing hind legs. The tadpole on page 19 is still older. It has grown front legs. Its fat body has become slender and its head more frog-like.

The body change is called metamorphosis (MET-uh-MORE-fo-sis). It takes all winter in the South and a year or more in the colder North.

This picture shows a close-up of a changing tadpole. Its front feet look like little hands. Its hind feet are webbed, for swimming. In back of its eye are dark gills for breathing underwater. But inside its body, it is growing lungs that will enable it to breathe air. Its intestines are changing, too. Soon it will eat animal foods instead of plants. Its metamorphosis will be complete when its tail has disappeared.

adult bullfrog

The change from bullfrog tadpole to adult takes one to three years. The metamorphosis is fastest in warm climates where the tadpole does not have to hibernate. After its metamorphosis, the frog must grow for two or three more years. Then it will be full grown and ready to mate.

A large, full-grown bullfrog may be eight inches long, from the snout to the place where its tail used to be.

Bullfrogs are often plain green above, with white under-parts. They may also be spotted, like the frog on the next page. The front feet look like four-fingered hands, while the hind feet are webbed for swimming. The powerful hind legs of the frog, when stretched out, are about eight inches long.

The male frog's throat contains a vocal sac. When the animal calls, it inflates the sac like a balloon, then forces the air out to make the noise.

The bullfrog in the picture is a female. We can tell because her ear—the round, flat thing just behind her eye —is about the same size as the eye. The male's ear is larger than the eye.

The bullfrog has good eyesight. It can see its prey above or below water. When it is submerged, its eyes are covered by transparent "window" eyelids.

Bullfrogs eat almost any animal they can swallow.

A hunting bullfrog is likely to wait very quietly until its prey comes near. It may sit on land or float in the water with just the upper part of its eyes and nostrils out in the air. When its prey comes near, the frog leaps or swims after it. Then it swallows the food whole, since it has no teeth.

Bullfrogs feed on fish, insects, and crayfish. They also eat ducklings, water snakes, and smaller frogs.

survival

The large, strong bullfrog has many enemies, even when it is full-grown. Snapping turtles, raccoons, opossums, mink, otters, hawks, owls, and large water snakes all devour bullfrogs when they can catch them.

The frog does its best to escape its enemies. It can leap great distances. And at the slightest sight of an enemy—even a shadow—it dives to the bottom of the water and hides until danger is past.

People like to hunt bullfrogs, too. Hunters go after the animals at night, when their loud croaks give away their hiding places. The entire frog is good to eat, but most people eat only the large hind legs. When they are fried, they taste like chicken.

Numbers of bullfrogs are raised for market on frog farms. Because of over-hunting, wild bullfrogs are becoming scarce in some places.

amphibians

Frogs belong to the animal group called amphibians. The word means "living in two worlds." It refers to the way these creatures begin life as water animals, then become air-breathers when they are adults.

Amphibians were the first animals with backbones to live on land.

The three kinds that are best known are frogs, toads, and salamanders.

Most frogs, like the bullfrog, have smooth, damp skins. They like to live near water and they are great jumpers. Toads are likely to have dry, bumpy skins. The "warts" are poison glands that protect the toad from being eaten by its enemies. Toads live away from water and do not jump very high. Salamanders, such as the newt, have long bodies and tails. They may live near water or in damp places on land.

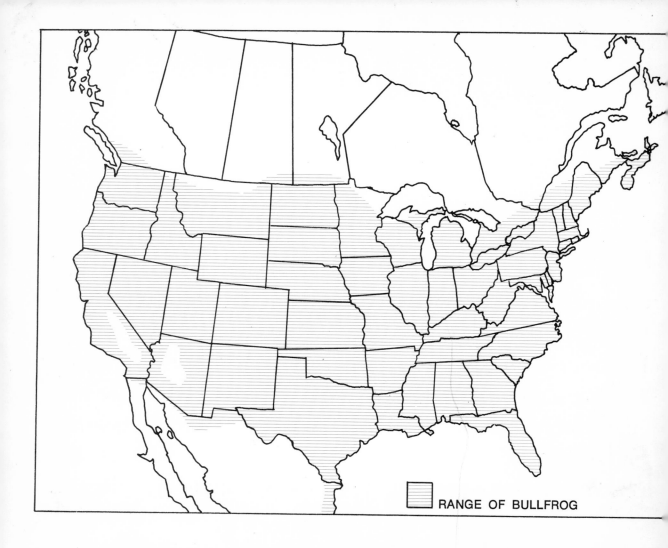

RANGE OF BULLFROG

range

Originally, the bullfrog lived in eastern North America from Nova Scotia to Florida and westward to the Great Plains. People who liked to eat frog legs took this animal to other parts of the continent and raised it in frog farms, or set it free in ponds. Because of man, the bullfrog is now found in almost all of the continental United States, in southern Canada, parts of Mexico, Cuba, and other places.

Other Creative Mini Books

Life Cycles

Life Cycle of a Bullfrog
Life Cycle of a Raccoon
Life Cycle of an Opossum
Life Cycle of a Moth
Life Cycle of a Rabbit
Life Cycle of a Fox
Life Cycle of a Turtle
Life Cycle of a Butterfly

World We Know

Fishes We Know
Birds We Know
Reptiles We Know
Mammals We Know
Insects We Know